Night Watch

JODI TOERING TANNYA HARRICKS

WALKER BOOKS
AND SUBSIDIARIES
LONDON • BOSTON • SYDNEY • AUCKLAND

Dusk whispers softly, soothing Day to slumber
as the last of Sunset's flames smoulder slowly skyward.

Tawny Frogmouth wakens.

With a task to complete and a journey ahead,
Tawny Frogmouth calls a drumming call.

Moon answers, rising gently over the
stubble to meet her and light the way.

It is time for the Night Watch.

Together, they fly.

Over oceans of wheat, swelling,
swaying in the breeze, they fly.

Quail waves quietly then nestles
down in the dust below the crop.

Over sparse eucalypts,
drenched in silver starlight, they fly.

Cockatoo peeps out of her hollow
then lulls her fledglings back to sleep.

Onwards through the bush, they fly.

Koala's baby has already drifted into dreamland, safe in the arms of their tree.

Under the black velvet sky
blanketing the earth, they fly.

Echidna bustles into his
hollow log and settles
down ’til morning.

Above the rocky outcrop jutting
high above the trees, they fly.

Wallaby gazes heavenward, shyly greeting
Moon, while her joey snuggles down in
the warmth and safety of her pouch.

Over great grasslands, stretching
infinite beneath the night, they fly.

Emu tucks his head beneath his feathers,
a small hill camouflaged against the earth.

Beyond vast spinifex plains, they fly.

Numbat snores, curled up with her brood
in a burrow below the warm red dirt.

Above the stony mountains,
bleached white in liquid moonlight, they fly.

Pygmy Possum, startled, scuttles
back into his crevice nest.

Down towards the winding river, rushing crystal clear, they fly.

Tawny Frogmouth glides, landing smoothly, and
becomes one with the branches of an ancient river gum.

With one last check to make tonight,
she peeks inside her twig-scramble nest.

Below Tawny Frogmouth's home, in a riverbank burrow set among the knotty roots, Platypus settles down to snooze, tail curled around her eggs.

Finally, Moon bids Tawny Frogmouth goodnight.

Dawn whispers softly, gently rousing Day, painting watercolour light across the land. Moon and Tawny Frogmouth drift off to sleep at last.

Their Night Watch is over for another night.

All is well.

For Derek - Night Skywatcher - J.T.

To parents and caregivers everywhere on the Night Watch - T.H.

Night Watch
first published in 2024
by Walker Books Australia Pty Ltd
Gadigal and Wangal Country
Locked Bag 22, Newtown
NSW 2042 Australia
www.walkerbooks.com.au

This edition published in 2025

Walker Books Australia acknowledges the Traditional Owners of the country on which we work, the Gadigal and Wangal peoples of the Eora Nation, and recognises their continuing connection to the land, waters and culture. We pay our respect to their Elders past and present.

A catalogue record for this book is available from the National Library of Australia

ISBN: 978 1 761601 68 2

The illustrations for this book were created using mixed media of acrylic paint, charcoal and graphite pencil with both chalk and oil pastel for detail.
Typeset in Old Claude
Design by Nicolette Treanor
Printed and bound in China

EU Authorized Representative: HackettFlynn Ltd,
36 Cloch Choirneal, Balrothery, Co. Dublin, K32 C942, Ireland.
EU@walkerpublishinggroup.com

10 9 8 7 6 5 4 3 2 1